More Fat-Free Recipes

More Fat-Free Recipes

Nevada Lampen

faber and faber

LONDON·BOSTON

First published in 1984
by Faber and Faber Limited
3 Queen Square London WC1N 3AU
Printed in Great Britain by
Redwood Burn Ltd, Trowbridge, Wiltshire
All rights reserved

British Library Cataloguing in Publication Data

Lampen, Nevada
  More fat-free recipes.
  1. Cookery 2. Fat-free diet
  I. Title
  641.5'638   TX717
  ISBN 0-571-13178-6

Contents

Introduction

For those who are familiar with my previous book, *Fat-Free Recipes*, cooking this way will by now have become a matter of routine, but I sincerely hope that those who have only just been introduced to a fat-free diet will find this book a help in preparing meals which, although rigidly within the concept of 'fat free', will prove satisfying and nourishing.

Many of the recipes would in the normal way contain fat or oil but, by careful adaptation, equally appetising dishes can be prepared and enjoyed.

It can be seen that I use powdered skimmed milk. The particular brand that I favour has as little as 0.15% fat, which is approximately 37 times less than normal milk. Although under the Trade Descriptions Act it has to be described as 'low fat', I should like to stress that this minuscule amount is accepted by the medical profession and adheres to the strict rules necessary to safeguard the health of fat-intolerant patients.

It is a good idea to plan menus ahead and to make up an adequate quantity of liquid skimmed milk, which can be used during the day for tea, coffee, custard, sauces and general cooking. I usually keep this covered in the fridge until required.

It is advisable to read the information given on all packet and canned foods to avoid using anything with fat or oil as there are, for example, gravy powders and stock cubes which contain fat and those which do not.

It is essential that bakeware is not greased so, if non-stick pans are not available, lining with rice paper or vegetable parchment is an easy way to overcome the problem.

My husband was placed on a fat-free diet by his specialist many years ago and very quickly became disinterested in food due to the rigidity of the diet.

It was this that prompted me to experiment with fat-free cooking to try to relieve the monotony for him and for many others in a similar position. This form of cooking is designed in particular for these people and, although the recipes are nutritious and interesting, the results should naturally not be compared to cooking with fat.

Although a certain amount of weight loss may result from following these recipes, they are not designed for those who wish to diet for this reason alone.

For patients who have also been advised to keep their sugar intake low, recipes which include sugar can of course be adjusted to taste and, where appropriate, artificial sweetener may be used.

For some years medical thinking has favoured the increased intake of dietary fibre in the fight against the so-called 'diseases of Western civilisation'. One of the bases of this type of diet is the use of wholemeal flour; although I have experimented with this flour I have not found it successful in fat-free cooking. It is a much heavier flour (than white) and, although there is no medical reason why it couldn't be used, experience has shown me that it does not give favourable results.

Dos and Don'ts

YOU MUST **NOT** EAT OR DRINK ANY OF THE FOLLOWING, OR ANYTHING CONTAINING THEM:

Butter
Cheese
Cream
Ordinary or Channel Islands milk
Margarine
Yolk of egg
Salad cream or mayonnaise
Kipper, mackerel or any other fatty or oily fish

Lard
Pork
Bacon
Ham
Sausage
Mutton
Liver
Suet

Pastry (unless made without fat)
Cake
Sponge containing any egg or egg powder
Biscuits: sweet, half sweet or Cornish wafer

Coconut
Nuts

Chocolate
Toffee
Ovaltine
Horlicks

NEVER FRY. Do NOT use vegetable oil or fat, 'edible' fat or olive oil.

Look at the list of contents of every tin or packet: if they include fat, vegetable oil or 'edible' fat, **DO NOT USE.**

YOU CAN EAT OR DRINK THE FOLLOWING:

Powdered skimmed milk containing no more than 0.15% fat
Tea and coffee
Alcohol
Cereals
Pastry without fat
Porridge
Bread, white or brown, fresh or toasted
Sugar
Boiled sweets

Jam
Honey
Marmalade

Jelly
Tinned fruit
'Milk' puddings and junket made with fat-free milk
Custard made with egg-free powder and fat-free milk

White of egg
Meringue

Biscuits: cracker or water biscuits
Potatoes: boiled, baked (jacket), or mashed with liquid skimmed milk. **NOT** roast, fried, chipped, mashed or treated with butter
Vegetables
Salad

Lean beef
Lean lamb
Lean tongue
Lean breast and leg of poultry.

White fish, boiled, grilled (no fat), or cooked in wine
Fat-free soups
Fruit, fresh or stewed

Marmite
Bovril
Mint sauce

Tomato ketchup
Fat-free pickles

By keeping to the rules of a fat-free diet it can be seen from the recipes included in this book that food can still be exciting and varied, but most of all thoroughly enjoyed.

Equivalent Weights and Measures

The American, and also the metric, equivalents of the British weights and measures used in these recipes are given below.

Liquid Measures

The fluid ounce (fl oz) is the same in both Britain and America

The British (or Imperial) pint	= 20 fl oz
The American pint	= 16 fl oz

Measuring cups (liquid measure)

British breakfast cup	= 10 fl oz ($\frac{1}{2}$ Imperial pint)
British teacup	= $6\frac{2}{3}$ fl oz ($\frac{1}{3}$ Imperial pint)
American standard cup	= 8 fl oz ($\frac{1}{2}$ American pint)

Standard measuring spoons (liquid measure)
The American standard tablespoon and standard teaspoon are slightly smaller than their British equivalents.

8 British standard tablespoons	= 5 fl oz
10 American standard tablespoons	= 5 fl oz
In each country, 3 teaspoons	= 1 tablespoon

1 British dessertspoon is approximately $\frac{1}{2}$ to $\frac{2}{3}$ of a tablespoon

Approximate Metric Equivalents

Liquid measures

1 fl oz	= 28 millilitres (ml)
1 British (Imperial) pint	= 570 ml
1 American pint	= 450 ml
1 litre	= $1\frac{3}{4}$ Imperial pints
	= $2\frac{1}{5}$ American pints

Weights

1 ounce (oz)	= 28 grams (g)
1 pound (lb) (16 oz)	= 454 g
1 kilogram (kg) (1000g)	= 2 lb 3 oz

Table of measurements for certain dry ingredients using American standard cup and tablespoon.

Ingredient	1 cup	Weight in ounces contained in: 1 level tablespoon
Sifted flour	4	$\frac{1}{4}$
Caster sugar	7	$\frac{1}{2}$
Confectioners' or icing sugar	$4\frac{1}{2}$	$\frac{1}{4}$
Syrup, treacle, molasses	12	$\frac{3}{4}$
Rice (whole grain)	$7\frac{1}{2}$	$\frac{1}{2}$
Currants	$5\frac{1}{2}$	—
Fresh breadcrumbs	$2\frac{1}{2}$	—
Cornstarch or cornflour	—	$\frac{1}{3}$

Savoury Dishes

Baked Whiting

Ingredients
½ lb whiting fillets
3 oz white breadcrumbs
small bunch of parsley, chopped
½ pint white sauce made with powdered skimmed milk and
   fish stock from recipe
4 tablespoons powdered skimmed milk
1 tablespoon sherry
2 tablespoons water + ¼ pint
½ teaspoon fish seasoning

Method
Cook the fish in a saucepan in ¼ pint of water and fish
seasoning. Mix breadcrumbs and powdered skimmed milk
with 2 tablespoons of water and place half in the bottom of
an ovenproof dish. Sprinkle over half the parsley. Strain fish
and reserve the stock for sauce. Flake the fish and replace in
the dish. Prepare the white sauce, using the fish stock and
sherry with a little more milk to make ½ pint sauce. Pour
gently over fish, cover with remaining parsley and
breadcrumb mixture. Bake in a preheated oven (375°F
(190°C) or Gas Mark 5) for 30 minutes, then brown under
the grill. Serve with boiled potatoes and peas. Serves two.

Chicken à l'Orange

Ingredients
2 leg and thigh chicken joints
½ teaspoon minced garlic or 1 clove, crushed (according to
    taste)
¼ lb breadcrumbs
1 oz powdered skimmed milk
1 small onion, grated
salt and pepper
few drops almond essence
1 small orange
1 dessertspoon honey

Method
Skin the chicken joints, score and sprinkle with garlic. Mix
the breadcrumbs, onion, powdered milk, salt and pepper
together with a little water and a few drops of almond
essence, and spread on to the base of a flat dish. Place
chicken portions on the top and season. Peel the orange,
removing pith and pips, and slice over joints. Dissolve
honey with a few drops of almond essence and spoon over
chicken. Cover with foil and cook in a preheated oven
(350°F (180°C) or Gas Mark 4) for 45 to 60 minutes or until
tender. Remove foil and brown under a grill. Serve with
boiled potatoes and a green vegetable. Serves two.

Chicken and Leek Casserole

Ingredients
2 leg and thigh chicken joints
½ lb leeks
½ large onion
4 level tablespoons powdered skimmed milk
1 level tablespoon plain flour
1 teaspoon dried mustard powder
salt and pepper
water

Method
Skin the chicken joints and remove any fat and season. Pressure cook or alternatively gently cook in a saucepan with a little water until tender. Wash and chop the leeks and onion and cook together in salted water until soft, then drain. Remove the joints from the pressure cooker or pan, reserving the stock, and place in the bottom of a casserole dish. Add onions and leeks. Pour the chicken liquid into a saucepan. Blend together the flour, powdered skimmed milk and mustard with a little of the stock. Bring remainder to the boil, then pour on to the blended mixture, stir well, return to the saucepan and boil for 1 minute. Season to taste and pour over the chicken and leeks. Allow to simmer for 25 to 30 minutes in a preheated oven (400°F (200°C) or Gas Mark 6). Serve with boiled potatoes and a green vegetable. Serves two.

Chicken and Mushroom Casserole

Ingredients
6 to 8 oz cooked chicken, diced and skin removed
¼ lb mushrooms
6 whole shallots, peeled
1 dessertspoon mixed dried peppers
½ lb fresh tomatoes or 8 oz tin tomatoes, discard liquid
¼ pint water
4 tablespoons liquid skimmed milk
3 tablespoons sherry
¼ teaspoon black pepper
pinch of salt
1 teaspoon curry powder
1 teaspoon tomato ketchup
1 dessertspoon cornflour

Method
Place the chicken in a casserole, add mushrooms, shallots
and dried peppers. Slice the tomatoes and arrange on top.
Mix the powdered milk with the water and curry powder,
ketchup, sherry and seasoning. Pour carefully over chicken
mixture. Cover casserole and bake in a preheated oven
(425°F (220°C) or Gas Mark 7) for 45 to 60 minutes.
Remove from the oven. Mix cornflour with a little water,
add to casserole and return to the oven for a further 15
minutes. Serve with boiled potatoes and a green vegetable.
Serves three.

Chicken Curry

Ingredients
6 oz chicken, cooked, skinned and minced
1 medium onion, peeled and sliced
½ lb fresh tomatoes, peeled and sliced, or 8 oz tin tomatoes
½ pint water
1 dessertspoon apricot jam
1 teaspoon brown sugar
1 dessertspoon Worcestershire sauce
1½ teaspoons curry powder
1 level teaspoon salt
shake of pepper

Method
Pour the water into a saucepan and add the onions and
tomatoes (if using tinned tomatoes, discard the liquid).
Bring to the boil and simmer until tender. Add the salt,
pepper and curry powder together with the jam, sugar,
sauce and minced chicken. Continue to simmer, stirring
occasionally, for 20 to 30 minutes until the liquid has been
absorbed and the flavours have combined. Serve on a bed of
boiled rice. Serves two.

Chicken Drumsticks in Aspic

Ingredients
6 chicken drumsticks, skinned
1 small onion, chopped
2 level teaspoons gelatine
¾ pint vegetable stock
few sprigs of parsley, chopped
salt and pepper

Method

Place the drumsticks in a casserole with the vegetable stock, onion and parsley and season to taste. Cover and cook in a preheated oven (400°F (200°C) or Gas Mark 6) for 35 to 40 minutes or until tender. Remove the casserole and strain the liquid. Dissolve the gelatine completely in the hot stock and reheat, but do not bring to the boil. Place the drumsticks in chosen dish, gently pour over the gelatine liquid and allow to cool. Place in refrigerator overnight. To serve, turn out and accompany with green salad. Serves three.

Mustardy Chicken

Ingredients

2 leg and thigh chicken joints, skinned
1 medium onion
4 tablespoons powdered skimmed milk
⅓ pint water
1 teaspoon made mustard
½ teaspoon salt
shake of pepper

Method

Place the chicken in a casserole. Mix together milk, mustard, salt and pepper and sprinkle over the joints. Peel and chop the onion finely and place on top. Add the water and cover. Bake in a preheated oven (400°F (200°C) or Gas Mark 6) for 1 hour or until tender. Serve on a bed of savoury rice or with boiled potatoes and a green vegetable. Serves two.

Savoury Chicken with Rice

Ingredients
2 leg and thigh chicken joints
3 medium tomatoes or 8 oz tin tomatoes, discard liquid
1 onion, sliced
¼ lb mixed frozen vegetables
1 dessertspoon dried mixed peppers
1 teaspoon Yorkshire relish (or an equivalent)
1 pint water
½ pint white sauce made with powdered skimmed milk
1 cup of long grain rice
salt
shake of black pepper

Method
Place the chicken joints, sliced onion, salt, black pepper and
1 pint of water into a saucepan, bring to the boil and simmer
gently until tender. Remove the skin and bones from the
chicken and cut into small pieces. Reserve the stock and
cool as quickly as possible. Place the chicken pieces in a
2-pint casserole with the mixed vegetables, tomatoes,
Yorkshire relish and peppers. Prepare the white sauce and
pour on to the chicken mixture. Stir well and cover. Place in
a preheated oven (350°F (180°C) or Gas Mark 3) and cook
for 1 hour. Meanwhile, skim off fat from cooled chicken
stock and make up to 1 pint with water and bring to the boil.
Add rice and simmer until tender. Strain. Serve chicken on
rice base. Serves two.

Turkey Pie

Ingredients
PASTRY
6 oz self-raising flour
3 tablespoons powdered skimmed milk
pinch of salt
water to mix

FILLING
$\frac{3}{4}$–1 lb cold cooked turkey, minced
4 oz button mushrooms, thinly sliced
small bunch of chives, chopped
$\frac{1}{2}$ pint white sauce made with powdered skimmed milk
salt and pepper

Method
To make the pastry, sieve all the dry ingredients into a bowl
and add a small quantity of water to make a stiff dough. Set
aside. Mix the turkey, mushrooms and chives together, add
the seasoning and stir in the white sauce. Roll out pastry on
a floured board. Flour an 8-inch pie plate and line with half
the pastry. Spread it with the turkey mixture and cover with
the remaining pastry. Brush with liquid skimmed milk and
cook on the top shelf of a preheated oven (400°F (200°C) or
Gas Mark 6) for 20 to 25 minutes. Serve with boiled
potatoes and a green vegetable. Serves four.

Lamb with Apricots

Ingredients
4 lean leg of lamb steaks
½ lb breadcrumbs
14½ oz tin apricots
small bunch parsley, chopped
1 medium onion, sliced
2 tablespoons powdered skimmed milk
salt and pepper

Method
Mix the breadcrumbs, powdered milk and parsley. Add a few finely chopped apricots, season and mix well. Trim the fat from the steaks. Place the breadcrumb mixture in a casserole and cover with sliced onion. Season steaks and place on top. Glaze with a little apricot syrup. Cover and bake in a preheated oven (400°F (200°C) or Gas Mark 6) for 1 hour or until tender. Remove from the oven and place the remaining apricots on top. Return uncovered to the oven for a further 15 minutes. Serve with vegetables in season. Serves four.

Lamb Cobbler

Ingredients
½ lb lean fillet of lamb
2 teaspoons Bovril
1 pint water
½ small turnip or swede
3 medium carrots
2 medium potatoes
¼ teaspoon black pepper
¼ teaspoon salt
1 teaspoon mint sauce
1 tablespoon flour

Topping
4 tablespoons self-raising flour
pinch of salt
4 tablespoons skimmed milk
1 clove garlic (according to taste)
1 teaspoon mint sauce
water to make a soft dough

Method
Make the stock by adding the boiling water to the Bovril and stir thoroughly. Cut meat into small pieces. Peel and chop vegetables and place with the meat in a 3-pint casserole dish. Add the salt and pepper and a teaspoon of mint sauce. Cover and cook in a preheated oven (350°F (180°C) or Gas Mark 4) for 1¼ to 1½ hours. Remove casserole from the oven. Mix the tablespoon of flour with a little cold water and add to the mixture to thicken. Meanwhile, make the topping by sieving the flour and salt together. Add the powdered skimmed milk, crushed garlic, mint sauce and enough water

to make a soft dough. Knead on a floured board and roll to ½-inch thickness. Cut into rounds and arrange around edge of casserole. Brush with liquid skimmed milk and return to oven and bake for 15 to 20 minutes or until nicely brown. Serves two.

Marinated Lamb Chops

Ingredients
4 lamb chops
1 dessertspoon honey
1 teaspoon mint sauce
1 tablespoon vinegar
2 teaspoons fresh or 1 teaspoon dried rosemary leaves
1 dessertspoon flour
1 dessertspoon gravy powder
salt and pepper

Method
Trim fat from the chops. Mix together the vinegar, honey, mint sauce, salt and pepper. Place chops in a flat dish and spoon the marinade over. Cover, and leave for at least an hour, turning the chops several times. Drain, and reserve juice. Sprinkle meat with rosemary. Preheat grill and gently cook chops on both sides. Meanwhile, mix together the flour and gravy powder with remaining marinade and make up to ½ pint with water. Bring gently to the boil. Place the chops in an ovenproof dish and add the gravy. Cover and place in a preheated oven (400°F (200°C) or Gas Mark 6) for 20 minutes. Serve with vegetables in season. Serves two.

Beef Cobbler

Ingredients
½ lb lean beef, cubed
½ lb tomatoes or 8 oz tin tomatoes
1 large onion, chopped
1 teaspoon brown sugar
1 teaspoon Bisto gravy powder
1 tablespoon plain flour
1 bay leaf
¼ pint water
salt and pepper

TOPPING
4 tablespoons self-raising flour
1 teaspoon mixed herbs
2 tablespoons powdered skimmed milk
½ level teaspoon salt
4 tablespoons water

Method
Mix flour, Bisto and seasoning together, thoroughly coat meat and place in a casserole. Add chopped onion, sugar, tomatoes and bay leaf together with ¼ pint of water, or juice if using tinned tomatoes. Cover and cook until tender in a preheated oven (400°F (200°C) or Gas Mark 6) for 1½ to 2 hours. To make topping, sieve the flour, milk and seasoning together, add mixed herbs and enough water to make a soft dough. Roll out to ½-inch thickness and cut into 2-inch rounds. Arrange these on top of the casserole. Brush with liquid skimmed milk. Bake uncovered for a further 20 minutes. Serve with boiled potatoes and a green vegetable. Serves two.

Country Garden Cottage Pie

Ingredients
¾–1 lb lean skirt of beef, minced
1 medium-sized leek
1 medium-sized potato
1 medium-sized parsnip
2 medium-sized carrots
½ medium-sized turnip
½ oz plain flour
½ pint water or stock
salt
shake of black pepper

Method
Place the meat in an ovenproof dish and add the sliced leek.
Mix stock or water with the flour and add to the meat.
Season to taste, cover and cook in a moderately hot oven
(400°F (200°C) or Gas Mark 6) for 1 hour until tender.
Meanwhile, chop the potato, turnip, parsnip and carrots,
place with salt and water in a saucepan and bring to the boil.
When cooked, strain and mash with a little liquid skimmed
milk and a shake of black pepper. Remove meat from oven
and spread with the mixed vegetables. Place under a grill
until golden brown. Serves four.

Cubed Beef with Breadcrumbs

Ingredients
1 lb beef skirt
½ lb tomatoes or 8 oz tin tomatoes, discard liquid
1 level tablespoon mixed dried peppers
small bunch chives, chopped
1 level tablespoon Bisto gravy powder
1 level tablespoon plain flour
1 rounded tablespoon breadcrumbs
1 pint Bovril stock
¼ teaspoon black pepper
pinch of salt

Method
Trim fat from meat and cut into small cubes. Mix the Bisto, flour and seasoning together and thoroughly coat meat. Place in a 2-pint casserole and sprinkle with breadcrumbs. Peel and slice the tomatoes, if fresh, or, if tinned, drain juice and place tomatoes on top of meat. Add the mixed peppers and chives. Gently pour over the Bovril stock, cover and bake in a preheated oven (375°F (190°C) or Gas Mark 5) for 1¼ hours. Serve with boiled potatoes and peas or cauliflower. Serves four.

Minced Meat Roly-poly

Ingredients
PASTRY
12 oz self-raising flour
6 level tablespoons powdered skimmed milk
pinch of salt

FILLING
1 lb lean skirt of beef
¼ teaspoon mixed herbs
1 small onion
salt and pepper

Method
To make the pastry, sieve flour, salt and milk together and add enough cold water to make a soft dough. Roll on a floured board into a rectangular shape. Mince the beef and onion together and add herbs and seasoning. Simmer gently in a little water for 30 minutes and allow to cool. Stir meat mixture thoroughly and spread over the pastry, leaving a border all round. Brush the border with liquid skimmed milk and roll, sealing the ends. Wrap in a floured cloth and then in tinfoil. Boil or steam for 1 hour. Serve with boiled vegetables – carrots, potatoes, cauliflower. Serves four.

Savoury Meat Sauce with Noodles

Ingredients
½ lb lean skirt of beef, minced
1 small onion, minced or finely chopped
½ lb tomatoes or 8 oz tin tomatoes, discard liquid
¼ pint Bovril stock
3 small carrots
2 oz mushrooms
1 teaspoon Worcestershire sauce
3 teaspoons brown sugar
2 teaspoons Bisto gravy powder
3 oz noodles
salt and pepper

Method
Peel and slice the carrots and mushrooms and cook in a saucepan with the beef, onion, tomatoes, sugar, Worcestershire sauce and Bovril stock until tender. Add the gravy powder to thicken just before serving. Place the noodles in a pan in 1½ pints cold water with ½ teaspoon salt and bring to the boil. Boil gently for about 15 minutes until tender. Drain and rinse with boiling water. Serve the meat sauce on a bed of noodles. Serves two.

Savoury Mincemeat Plait

Ingredients
PASTRY
4 rounded tablespoons self-raising flour
2 rounded tablespoons powdered skimmed milk
¼ teaspoon salt
water

FILLING
½ lb lean skirt or chuck beef, minced
1 small onion
1 dessertspoon mixed dried peppers (optional)
1 medium tomato, peeled and sliced
¼ pint Bovril stock including ½ teaspoon flour
salt and pepper

Method
Place beef and onion in a saucepan with the dried peppers and sliced tomato. Add the Bovril stock and seasoning and cook slowly until tender. Allow to cool. Meanwhile, sieve

the flour, powdered skimmed milk and salt and add enough water to make a soft pastry dough. Roll out into an oblong. Place the cooled meat mixture down the centre of the pastry. Cut pastry at 1-inch intervals to within an inch of the filling. Brush with liquid skimmed milk, fold strips of pastry alternately from each side over the filling. Brush over with skimmed milk and place on a non-stick baking tray. Cook on the middle shelf of a preheated oven (400°F (200°C) or Gas Mark 6) for 20 to 25 minutes or until nicely brown. Cover with a clean cloth to steam. Serves two.

Sea Pie Pudding (Seasoned Pudding)

Ingredients
PASTRY
6 rounded tablespoons self-raising flour
3 rounded tablespoons powdered skimmed milk
$\frac{1}{4}$ teaspoon salt
water to mix

FILLING
$\frac{1}{2}$–$\frac{3}{4}$ lb lean beef or skirt, finely cut
2 large potatoes
2 medium-sized onions
1 teaspoon Bisto gravy powder
$\frac{1}{4}$ pint water
salt and pepper

Method
Place meat, shredded potatoes and onions in a saucepan with water and seasoning and bring to the boil. Simmer

until tender. Mix the gravy powder with a little water and add to the saucepan and reheat. Allow to cool. Meanwhile make pastry by sieving all dry ingredients into a bowl and adding a small quantity of water to make a stiff dough. Generously flour the board and roll out pastry to line a 1½-pint basin, reserving enough for pastry lid. Pour meat mixture into basin and cover with remaining pastry. Cover with a floured cloth or tinfoil and secure firmly. Boil or steam for 1 hour. Serve with vegetables. Serves four.

Steak and Kidney Pudding

Ingredients
PASTRY
6 rounded tablespoons self-raising flour
3 rounded tablespoons powdered skimmed milk
¼ teaspoon salt
water to mix

FILLING
1 lb skirt of beef or chuck steak
2 small kidneys, cored
2 oz mushrooms, sliced (optional)
1 teaspoon plain flour
1 dessertspoon Bisto gravy powder
¼ teaspoon marjoram
salt and pepper
water

Method
Cut the meat and kidney into small cubes. Season and cook in a pressure cooker together with the mushrooms and

enough water to cover, or cook until tender in a saucepan. Thicken by mixing flour, Bisto and marjoram together with a little water, add to the saucepan and gently reheat. Allow to cool. Meanwhile, make pastry by sieving all dry ingredients into a bowl and adding a small amount of water to make a stiff dough. Generously flour board and roll out pastry to line a 1½-pint basin, reserving enough for pastry lid. Spoon in the meat mixture and cover with remaining pastry. Cover with cloth or tinfoil, secure firmly and boil or steam for 1 hour. Serve with boiled potatoes and cauliflower. Serves four.

Stuffed Beef Rolls

Ingredients
½ lb lean best stewing beef cut into a thin slice
4 oz breadcrumbs
½ pint Bovril or other meat stock
1 teaspoon lemon juice
1 tablespoon powdered skimmed milk
small bunch parsley, chopped
¼ teaspoon mixed herbs
¼ teaspoon black pepper
salt
water to mix

Method
Cut the slice of meat into 4 equal portions and beat until flat. Mix the breadcrumbs, parsley, herbs, powdered milk and seasonings together and add the water and lemon juice to bind. Divide into equal portions and spread on to the

meat. Roll up and secure with wooden cocktail sticks or string. Place the stuffed rolled meat into a casserole, pour over stock, cover and cook in a preheated oven (400°F (200°C) or Gas Mark 6) for 35 to 40 minutes. Serve with mashed potatoes and a green vegetable. Serves two.

Pizza

Ingredients
BASE
4 tablespoons self-raising flour
½ teaspoon baking powder
1½ teaspoons dried mustard powder
1 heaped tablespoon powdered skimmed milk
liquid skimmed milk to mix
pinch of salt

TOPPING
¼ lb tongue
8 oz tin tomatoes
½ medium onion, grated
½ teaspoon sugar
1 tablespoon tomato purée
½ teaspoon mixed herbs
1 teaspoon made mustard
salt and pepper
parsley to garnish

Method
Place tomatoes, onion, sugar and purée into a non-stick saucepan and season to taste. Simmer, stirring occasionally.

Meanwhile, prepare the scone base by sieving all dry ingredients into a bowl and adding liquid milk to bind. Divide into 2 and roll into rounds of 8-inch diameter. Place on a floured non-stick baking tray and spread with made-up mustard. Add the cooked tomato mixture to within $\frac{1}{2}$ inch of edges. Mince tongue and add equal amounts to each scone. Sprinkle with herbs and cook in a preheated oven (400°F (200°C) or Gas Mark 6) for 15 to 20 minutes. Garnish with parsley and serve immediately. Serves two.

Meat Sauce with Pasta Shells

Ingredients
$\frac{1}{2}$ lb lean minced skirt of beef
2 sticks celery
$\frac{1}{4}$ lb mushrooms
1 large onion
2 medium carrots
$\frac{1}{2}$ lb fresh or 8 oz tin tomatoes
2 teaspoons Worcestershire sauce
1 oz flour
1 teaspoon Bovril
$\frac{1}{2}$ pint water
$\frac{1}{4}$ teaspoon salt
$\frac{1}{4}$ teaspoon black pepper
4–6 oz pasta shells
2 pints water

Method
Peel and slice onion, carrots, celery and mushrooms and skin tomatoes if fresh. Make Bovril stock. Place these

ingredients together with the meat seasoning and sauce in a pressure cooker or saucepan and cook until tender. If using tinned tomatoes, drain and add to the mixture. Mix the flour with a little water and add to the meat sauce. Bring back to the boil, cover and gently simmer. Meanwhile, bring 2 pints of salted water to the boil, add the pasta shells, return to the boil and simmer for 12 to 15 minutes. Adjust seasoning and serve the meat sauce on a warmed dish with the pasta shells. Serves two to three.

Spaghetti Bolognese

Ingredients
½ lb lean minced skirt of beef
1 small onion
1 clove garlic (according to taste)
pinch mixed herbs
6 oz mushrooms
¾ pint water
2 heaped teaspoons tomato purée
2 teaspoons dark brown sugar
salt and pepper
4–6 oz spaghetti

Method
Place the minced beef in a pressure cooker or saucepan with water, salt and pepper and cook until tender. Meanwhile, peel the onion and garlic and chop into small pieces. Wash and slice mushrooms and add with the onion and garlic to the meat. Stir frequently to prevent sticking. Finally, add the sugar, herbs and purée and cook gently for a further 20

to 30 minutes or until the mixture thickens. Bring a saucepan of salted water to the boil, add the spaghetti and bring back to the boil. Simmer until tender, drain and serve with the Bolognese sauce in a warmed dish. Serves two to three.

Tongue, Yorkshire Style

Ingredients
½ lb tongue
4 tablespoons self-raising flour
2 tablespoons powdered skimmed milk
6 tablespoons cold water
½ teaspoon mustard powder
pinch of salt

Method
Sieve together the flour, milk, salt and mustard powder. Add the water and beat thoroughly until a smooth consistency is formed. Mince the tongue. Pour half the mixture into an ovenproof or non-stick dish. Sprinkle the tongue over the top of the mixture and pour on the remaining batter. Bake in a preheated oven (375°F (190°C) or Gas Mark 5) for 35 to 40 minutes. Serve with boiled potatoes and a green vegetable. A little gravy may be added to the meat if desired. Serves two.

Bubble and Squeak

Ingredients
4 oz boiled potatoes
4 oz boiled turnips
4 oz boiled cabbage
1 heaped tablespoon chutney
extra seasoning optional
carrots or beans may be substituted

Method
Mash the vegetables together with a little extra seasoning if required. Stir in the chutney and cook gently in a non-stick frying pan, turning until golden brown on both sides. Serve with cold chicken, lamb or beef. Serves two.

Savoury Jacket Potatoes

Ingredients
6 medium potatoes, scrubbed
½ lb lean minced skirt of beef
1 medium onion, minced
small bunch parsley, chopped
salt and pepper
6 skewers

Method
Place a skewer lengthwise through each potato and wrap separately in tinfoil. Bake on a tray in a preheated oven (450°F (230°C) or Gas Mark 8) for about 45 minutes. Meanwhile, cook the minced beef, onion and seasoning in a

little water until tender. When potatoes are soft, scoop out the insides and mix with the minced beef and onion. Fill each potato with the mixture, sprinkle with chopped parsley and replace in the oven for a further 15 minutes. Serve as a supper snack or for lunch with a green salad. Serves three.

Tomato and Egg Nests

Ingredients
1 lb boiled potatoes
1 large tomato
1 large egg white
small sprig parsley
small amount liquid skimmed milk
salt and pepper

Method
Mash the boiled potatoes with a sprinkling of pepper and some liquid skimmed milk. Place in a piping bag, or use a spoon, and form 6 rings of potato on a non-stick baking tray. Peel the tomato and chop very small. Beat the egg white and seasoning, add the tomato and mix. Spoon the mixture into the centre of the potato rings and put under a hot grill until golden brown. Sprinkle with parsley. Serve hot as a supper snack or for lunch with a green salad. Serves two.

Quick Potato Salad

Ingredients
4 small new potatoes
3 tablespoons powdered skimmed milk
2–3 tablespoons white vinegar
1 teaspoon made mustard
1 teaspoon caster sugar
small bunch chives, chopped
¼ teaspoon salt
¼ teaspoon pepper

Method
Mix together thoroughly milk, sugar, salt, pepper and mustard with the white vinegar. Dice potatoes into small cubes and add with the chives to the mixture, ensuring all are thoroughly mixed. Cover and chill before use. Serves two.

Sweets: Meringue Topped

Crunchy Meringue Pie

Ingredients
3 oz cornflakes
1 tablespoon syrup
1½ tablespoons custard powder
1½ level tablespoons sugar
½ pint liquid skimmed milk
2 tablespoons marmalade
glacé cherries for decoration

TOPPING
2 standard (No. 3 size) egg whites
2 tablespoons caster sugar

Method
Crush the cornflakes and place in a saucepan with the syrup.
Stir over a low heat until cornflakes are thoroughly coated.
Spread the mixture into an ovenproof dish, pressing well
down with a spoon. Meanwhile, make the custard and pour
over the cornflake mixture levelling with a palette knife.
When cold, spread with the marmalade. To make the

meringue, whisk the egg whites until stiff and gradually fold in the caster sugar. Arrange on top of the pie, decorate with cherries and bake in a preheated oven (375°F (190°C) or Gas Mark 5) for 10 minutes. When cool will keep in a refrigerator for three or four days. Serves four to six.

Date and Meringue Pie

Ingredients
PASTRY
4 rounded tablespoons self-raising flour
2 rounded tablespoons powdered skimmed milk
1 dessertspoon caster sugar
pinch of salt
water

FILLING
1 tablespoon brandy
6 oz stoned dates

TOPPING
2 standard (No. 3 size) egg whites
3 oz caster sugar
2 oz ground rice

Method
Make the pastry by sieving together the dry ingredients and adding enough water to form a soft dough. Place the chopped dates in a basin, cover with hot water and leave to soak for 15 minutes. Line a flan dish with pastry. Drain surplus water from dates, add brandy and beat with a fork.

Spread carefully on the pastry case. Whisk the egg whites until stiff, gradually adding the sugar, and fold in the ground rice. Cover the dates with meringue mixture and bake in a preheated oven (400°F (200°C) or Gas Mark 6) for 10 minutes, reducing heat to moderately low (300°F (150°C) or Gas Mark 2) for a further 20 minutes or until golden brown. Serves four to six.

Date, Apple and Rice Meringue

Ingredients
2 large cooking apples
3 tablespoons caster sugar (1)
¼ pint + 1 pint water
½ cup pudding rice
2 large (No. 1 size) egg whites
3 tablespoons caster sugar (2)
½ teaspoon cinnamon
4 oz stoned dates, chopped

Method
Put the rice into a saucepan with 1 pint water and 1 tablespoon sugar. Bring to the boil and simmer until soft. Remove from heat and drain. Peel, core and dice apples and place in a saucepan together with dates, 2 tablespoons sugar and ¼ pint water and boil until tender. Add the cinnamon. Stir the rice into the apple mixture and place in an ovenproof serving dish. Whisk the egg whites until stiff, adding the 3 remaining tablespoons sugar gradually between each beating. Spread on the apple mixture and bake in a preheated oven (350°F (180°C) or Gas Mark 4) until brown. Serves four to six.

Lemon Meringue Pie

Ingredients
PASTRY
4 rounded tablespoons self-raising flour
2 rounded tablespoons powdered skimmed milk
pinch of salt
water

FILLING
$\frac{1}{4}$ lemon jelly
1 level tablespoon custard powder
1 tablespoon sugar
juice of $\frac{1}{2}$ fresh lemon

TOPPING
1 large (No. 1 size) egg white
1 level tablespoon caster sugar

Method
Prepare jelly and custard in normal way and allow to cool
but not to set. Meanwhile, make the pastry by sieving the
dry ingredients together, adding enough water to form a
soft dough. Line a non-stick flan dish with pastry and bake
blind in a preheated oven (425°F (220°C) or Gas Mark 7) for
10 to 15 minutes. Mix the jelly and custard together and add
the lemon juice. Place on top of the pastry. Whisk egg white
until it stands in peaks, gradually adding the sugar. Cover
pie with meringue topping and return to the oven (300°F
(150°C) or Gas Mark 2) for 25 to 30 minutes. Serves four to
six.

Mandarin and Rice Meringue

Ingredients
11 oz tin of mandarin oranges
¾ cup rice
1½ pints water
2 tablespoons caster sugar
4 tablespoons powdered skimmed milk
small piece of angelica for decoration

TOPPING
2 large (No. 1 size) egg whites
2 tablespoons caster sugar
1 teaspoon ground rice

Method
Cook the rice in 1½ pints water with 2 tablespoons sugar until tender, and strain. Drain mandarins, reserving juice, and place segments on the base of an ovenproof dish, setting aside 6 segments for decoration. Mix the rice, juice and powdered skimmed milk together thoroughly and place on the fruit. To make the meringue, whisk the egg whites until stiff and standing in peaks. Gradually fold in the sugar and finally add the ground rice. Spread the meringue over the rice and bake in a preheated oven (375°F (190°C) or Gas Mark 5) for 15 to 20 minutes. Decorate with the reserved mandarins and angelica to form florets. Serves four.

Mincemeat Meringue Flan

Ingredients

PASTRY
4 rounded tablespoons self-raising flour
2 rounded tablespoons powdered skimmed milk
1 dessertspoon caster sugar
pinch of salt
water

MINCEMEAT
1 apple, peeled and cored
2 tablespoons brown sugar
1 tablespoon sultanas and currants mixed
1 tablespoon cherries, chopped
1 oz mixed peel
1 tablespoon brandy, whisky or sherry
1 tablespoon marmalade
1 level teaspoon mixed spice
shake of nutmeg
1 rounded tablespoon powdered skimmed milk

TOPPING
2 standard (No. 3 size) egg whites
3 oz caster sugar

Method
To make the mincemeat, grate the apple and cook with the sugar until tender. When cold stir in all the other ingredients leaving the powdered milk until last. Make the pastry by sieving the dry ingredients together and adding enough water to make a soft dough. Line a flan dish and cover with mincemeat. Whisk the egg whites until soft, gradually

folding in the sugar. Cover the mincemeat with the meringue and cook (400°F (200°C) or Gas Mark 6) for 10 minutes, reducing heat (300°F (150°C) or Gas Mark 2) for a further 20 minutes or until golden brown. Serves four.

Rhubarb and Apple Flan

Ingredients
BASE
3 oz crushed cornflakes
1½ oz icing sugar
1 large (No. 1 size) egg white

FILLING
½ lb rhubarb
1 large eating apple
2 tablespoons sugar
2 tablespoons water

TOPPING
1 large (No. 1 size) egg white
2 level tablespoons caster sugar

Method
Wash rhubarb and cut into 1-inch pieces. Peel, core and shred the apple and place in a saucepan with the rhubarb, sugar and water. Boil gently until tender and allow to cool. Mix the cornflakes and icing sugar with the beaten egg white and spread on to the base of a flan dish (lined if necessary). Bake in a preheated oven (350°F (180°C) or Gas Mark 4) for 10 to 15 minutes. Remove from the oven, cover with

rhubarb and apple mixture. Prepare topping by whisking egg white until stiff, gradually adding the sugar a little at a time. Top the fruit with the meringue, return to the oven and cook until golden brown. Serves four.

Semolina and Peach Meringue

Ingredients
1 pint liquid skimmed milk
4 level tablespoons semolina
3 tablespoons caster sugar
14½ oz tin of peaches
2 oz raisins
2 large (No. 1 size) egg whites
3 oz caster sugar

Method
Heat the milk. Stir in the semolina and 3 tablespoons sugar and boil until the mixture thickens, reduce heat and cook gently for 3 to 4 minutes. Turn into suitable ovenproof dish. Drain peaches and reserve juice. Place the raisins into a saucepan with 4 tablespoons of fruit juice and boil gently until the liquid has been absorbed into the fruit. Liquidise the peaches or mash with a fork and stir into the semolina together with the sweetened raisins. Mix well. Whisk the egg whites until stiff, gradually folding in remaining 3 tablespoons caster sugar. Spread over the mixture and bake in a preheated oven (350°F (180°C) or Gas Mark 5) for 10 to 15 minutes. Can be eaten hot or cold. Serves four to six.

Spicy Apple Meringue

Ingredients

PASTRY
4 tablespoons self-raising flour
2 tablespoons powdered skimmed milk
1 dessertspoon caster sugar
pinch of salt
water

FILLING
¾ lb apples, peeled and cored
2 oz raisins
3 oz brown sugar
½ teaspoon cinnamon
3 tablespoons water
glacé cherries for decoration

TOPPING
2 large (No. 1 size) egg whites
3 level tablespoons caster sugar

Method
Make the pastry by sieving the dry ingredients together and adding enough water to form a soft dough. Slice the apple and put in a saucepan with sugar, raisins and water and bring to the boil. Simmer until tender, allow to cool and stir in the cinnamon. Meanwhile, line a flan dish with the pastry and bake blind in a preheated oven (375°F (190°C) or Gas Mark 5) for 10 to 15 minutes. Remove from oven and cover with apple mixture. Whisk the egg whites until stiff, gradually adding the sugar. Spoon the meringue over the apple and decorate with cherries. Return to the oven for a

further 10 minutes or until golden brown. Serves four to six.

Sultana and Rice Meringue

Ingredients
¾ cup pudding rice
2 oz Demerara or light brown sugar
2 level tablespoons caster sugar
4 oz sultanas
¼ pint liquid powdered skimmed milk
½ teaspoon vanilla essence
2 large (No. 1 size) egg whites

Method
Boil rice in lightly salted water until tender. Strain and add the fruit, brown sugar and milk. Return to the heat and simmer gently for 15 minutes. Cool and turn into suitable dish. Whisk the egg whites until stiff and standing in peaks, gradually adding the caster sugar and essence. Spread on top of the rice mixture. Place in a preheated oven (300°F (150°C) or Gas Mark 2) for approximately 30 minutes or until golden brown. Serves four.

Sweets: Steamed or Grilled

Apple Crisp

Ingredients
½ lb cooking apples, peeled and sliced
2 tablespoons orange squash
1 tablespoon caster sugar

Topping
¼ lb fine breadcrumbs
1 tablespoon syrup, from a warm spoon

Method
Place the apple in a saucepan with the orange squash and sugar and bring to the boil slowly. When cooked, spoon into suitable dish. Put the breadcrumbs into a saucepan with the syrup and heat slowly, stirring until the syrup is absorbed into the breadcrumbs. Turn on to the apple mixture and place under the grill to brown. Serve immediately. Serves two.

Crêpes Suzette with Orange and Lemon Sauce

Ingredients
2 rounded tablespoons self-raising flour
1 rounded tablespoon caster sugar
1 rounded tablespoon powdered skimmed milk
2 tablespoons liquid skimmed milk
1 teaspoon custard powder
white of 1 large (No. 1 size) egg
pinch of salt

Filling
2 dessertspoons lemon jelly marmalade
2 rounded tablespoons powdered skimmed milk
1 teaspoon Grand Marnier

Sauce
juice of ½ orange
juice of ½ lemon
1 tablespoon caster sugar

Method
Sieve all dry ingredients together into a mixing bowl, make a well and add egg white and enough liquid milk to make a smooth batter. Divide mixture into 2 and pour half into a non-stick pan. Swivel the pan so that the mixture covers the base and cook over medium heat for 2 minutes each side until nicely brown. Cook the remaining batter in the same way and keep warm in the oven. Mix the marmalade together with powdered skimmed milk until creamy, add the Grand Marnier and stir thoroughly. Spread mixture over pancakes and fold over, returning them to warm oven.

Make sauce by boiling juices together with sugar in a small saucepan until syrupy. Pour over pancakes and sprinkle with extra Grand Marnier if desired. Serve immediately. Serves two.

Lemon Pudding with Lemon Sauce

Ingredients
4 rounded tablespoons plain flour
2 level tablespoons caster sugar
2 rounded tablespoons powdered skimmed milk
1½ level teaspoons Golden Raising Powder
pinch of salt
2 tablespoons lemon marmalade
grated rind and juice of 1 small lemon
4–6 tablespoons liquid skimmed milk

Sauce
3 oz caster sugar
2 level tablespoons custard powder
1 large (No. 1 size) egg white
rind and juice of 1 small lemon
¼ pint water

Method
Sieve all dry ingredients into a bowl, add grated lemon rind, lemon juice and liquid milk. Stir thoroughly. Place the marmalade in the bottom of a non-stick basin and pour the mixture over. Secure with greaseproof paper or tinfoil and boil or steam for 1 hour. To make the sauce, put the custard powder and sugar into a saucepan and gradually add the

water. Bring to the boil, stirring all the time. Remove from heat. Whisk the egg white until stiff and add to the mixture. Grate the lemon rind and stir in with the juice. Beat well and return to heat. Serves four.

Marmalade and Ginger Pudding

Ingredients
2–3 tablespoons marmalade
4 tablespoons self-raising flour
2 tablespoons powdered skimmed milk
1 teaspoon ground ginger
2 level tablespoons brown sugar, moist
1 dessertspoon syrup from a warmed spoon
¼ teaspoon bicarbonate soda
little liquid skimmed milk
pinch of salt

Method
Sieve the flour, milk, bicarbonate, ginger and salt together. Stir in the sugar and syrup and add enough liquid milk to form a soft consistency. Place the marmalade in the bottom of a non-stick basin and pour sponge mixture over. Cover with a floured cloth or tinfoil. Secure well and boil or steam for 1 hour. Serve with custard. Serves four.

Orange and Marshmallow Dessert

Ingredients
11 oz tin mandarin oranges
2 oz marshmallows, halved
2 oz ground rice
¾ pint liquid skimmed milk
2 tablespoons caster sugar

Method
Drain oranges and reserve the juice. Arrange the fruits in the base of an ovenproof dish. Using the juice, make up to 1 pint with the liquid milk, pour into a saucepan and bring to the boil stirring in the ground rice and sugar. Continue to stir for 2 to 3 minutes or until the ground rice is cooked. Pour carefully over the oranges and arrange the marshmallows on top. Place under a medium grill to brown. Serves four.

Orange Marmalade Pudding

Ingredients
1 medium orange
3 tablespoons orange marmalade
4 tablespoons plain flour
1½ level teaspoons Golden Raising Powder
2 level tablespoons caster sugar (for dredging orange slices)
pinch of salt
2 rounded tablespoons powdered skimmed milk
4–6 tablespoons liquid skimmed milk

Method

Take 1 tablespoon of marmalade and rub all over the inside of a 1½-pint pudding basin. Peel the orange, remove all the pith and cut into thin rounds, discarding any pips. Arrange the orange slices in the bottom and around the sides of the basin after dredging each slice with sugar. Sieve all dry ingredients together into a bowl, add the liquid milk and mix thoroughly, adding 1 tablespoon of marmalade to the mixture. Spoon any juice and the remaining marmalade over the arranged fruit in the basin. Next carefully pour over the sponge mixture. Secure with tinfoil and steam or boil for 1 hour. Serve with custard. Serves four.

Pineapple Pudding with Pineapple Sauce

Ingredients
4 rounded tablespoons plain flour
2 level tablespoons caster sugar
2 rounded tablespoons powdered skimmed milk
1½ level teaspoons Golden Raising Powder
2 tablespoons crushed pineapple
little pineapple juice
pinch of salt

SAUCE
1 dessertspoon cornflour
1 tablespoon pineapple jam
1 dessertspoon sugar
4 tablespoons pineapple juice made up to ¼ pint with water

Method

Sieve all dry ingredients into a bowl. Stir in crushed pineapple and mix thoroughly with a little juice. Place in a non-stick basin and cover with a floured cloth or tinfoil and boil or steam for 1 hour. Meanwhile, prepare the pineapple sauce by putting juice, water, jam and sugar into a saucepan. Bring slowly to the boil, reserving a little water to mix the cornflour into a smooth paste in a basin. When the syrup has boiled, pour on to the cornflour and stir well. Return to the saucepan and bring back to the boil. Simmer for a few minutes. Serve pudding hot with sauce and custard if desired. Serves two to three.

Rice Caramel

Ingredients

1 cup short grain rice
1½ pints water
2 tablespoons custard powder
3 tablespoons caster sugar
2 tablespoons Demerara sugar
1 pint liquid skimmed milk
little nutmeg
pinch of salt

Method

Add rice to boiling salted water with 1 tablespoon caster sugar and simmer until soft. Strain and rinse well with hot water to separate the grains. Put the custard powder and remaining caster sugar in a basin and add a little milk taken from the pint to mix and form a paste. Bring the rest of the milk to the boil, add to custard powder, stir thoroughly and return to the heat until mixture thickens. Stir in the cooked rice and place in an ovenproof dish. Sprinkle with nutmeg and Demerara sugar. Place under grill until brown. Serves four to six.

Sweets: Baked

Apple and Almond Flan

Ingredients
PASTRY
4 tablespoons self-raising flour
2 tablespoons powdered skimmed milk
1 dessertspoon caster sugar
1 teaspoon almond essence
water

FILLING
1 lb cooking apples, peeled and cored, and }
3 tablespoons sugar

      or

14 oz tin apple pie filling }
3 tablespoons water

LATTICE WORK
1 tablespoon plain flour
1 tablespoon sugar
1 teaspoon almond essence

Method
Make the pastry by sieving the dry ingredients together and
adding the almond essence and enough water to form a soft

dough. Line a flan dish with the pastry. If using fresh apple, stew with sugar and allow to cool. Cover pastry base with apple. Blend the flour, sugar and almond essence together with enough water to make a running consistency and pour over apple to make a lattice design. Bake in a preheated oven (425°F (220°C) or Gas Mark 7) for 20 to 25 minutes. Serves four.

Apple Strudel

Ingredients
PASTRY
4 rounded tablespoons self-raising flour
2 rounded tablespoons powdered skimmed milk
3 teaspoons caster sugar
pinch of salt

FILLING
2 rounded tablespoons Demerara sugar
3 oz raisins
2 medium apples
$\frac{1}{4}$ teaspoon cinnamon
$\frac{1}{2}$ teaspoon mixed spice

Method
Sieve flour, milk and salt together, stir in 2 teaspoons caster sugar and add enough water to make a soft dough. Generously flour board and roll out pastry to form an oblong. Peel, core and grate apples finely and spread over the pastry leaving $\frac{3}{4}$-inch border. Sprinkle with the Demerara sugar and add the fruit and spices, pressing well

into the pastry. Dampen the edges, roll up and place on a non-stick swiss-roll tin. Sprinkle with remaining caster sugar and bake on the middle shelf of a preheated oven (375°F (190°C) or Gas Mark 5) for 30 to 35 minutes. Serve warm. Serves two to three.

Bakewell Tart

Ingredients
PASTRY
4 rounded tablespoons self-raising flour
2 rounded tablespoons powdered skimmed milk
1 dessertspoon caster sugar
pinch of salt
water

FILLING
1 dessertspoon custard powder
4 oz breadcrumbs
3 oz caster sugar
1 large (No. 1 size) egg white
2 tablespoons powdered skimmed milk
3 tablespoons strawberry or raspberry jam
2 tablespoons liquid skimmed milk
½ teaspoon almond essence

Method
Make the pastry by sieving the dry ingredients together and adding enough water to form a soft dough. Place the sugar, powdered milk and custard powder into a bowl and add the liquid milk and beat until creamy. Gradually beat in the egg

white and essence and finally stir in the breadcrumbs. Line a flan dish with pastry, spread with jam and cover with breadcrumb mixture. Bake in a preheated oven (400°F (200°C) or Gas Mark 6) for 20 to 25 minutes until golden brown. Serves four.

Custard Tart

Ingredients
PASTRY
4 rounded tablespoons self-raising flour
2 rounded tablespoons powdered skimmed milk
1 dessertspoon caster sugar
pinch of salt
water

FILLING
4 level tablespoons custard powder
2 level tablespoons sugar
$\frac{3}{4}$ pint liquid skimmed milk
3 tablespoons strawberry or raspberry jam
angelica for decoration

Method
To make the pastry sieve the flour, milk and salt together, add the sugar and mix. Add enough water to make a soft dough. Roll out pastry on a generously floured surface and line a non-stick flan dish and bake in a preheated oven (400°F (200°C) or Gas Mark 6) for 10 to 15 minutes or until firm. Meanwhile, make the custard and cool, stirring

frequently to prevent a skin from forming. When the flan ring is cold, spread with jam and top with custard. Decorate with angelica. Serves four to six.

Egg Custard

Ingredients
2 or 3 large (No. 1 size) egg whites
1 pint liquid skimmed milk
2 rounded tablespoons caster sugar
2 rounded tablespoons custard powder
grated nutmeg

Method
Whisk together the egg whites, custard powder, sugar and a little milk taken from the pint until frothy. Add remaining milk and whisk again. Pour into an ovenproof dish and sprinkle with nutmeg. Bake in a preheated oven (400°F (200°C) or Gas Mark 6) for 1 hour stirring several times during cooking. Serves four.

Fruited Bread Pie

PASTRY
4 rounded tablespoons self-raising flour
2 rounded tablespoons powdered skimmed milk
1 dessertspoon caster sugar
pinch of salt
water

FILLING
4 slices bread, trimmed
2 tablespoons brown sugar
½ teaspoon rum essence
¼ pint liquid skimmed milk
2 tablespoons currants
1 tablespoon sultanas
red or green cherries for decoration

ICING
4 tablespoons icing sugar, sifted
1 dessertspoon warm water

Method
Make the pastry by sieving all the dry ingredients together
and adding enough warm water to form a soft dough. Cut
the bread into small pieces and add the sugar, currants and
sultanas. Stir in the rum essence and liquid milk. Leave to
soak for 15 minutes, occasionally mashing with a fork. Line
a flan dish with the pastry and cover with the bread mixture.
Bake in a preheated oven (400°F (200°C) or Gas Mark 6) for
15 minutes, reducing heat (300°F (150°C) or Gas Mark 2)
for a further 10 minutes. Allow to cool. Mix the sieved icing
sugar with the warm water and spread over the pie.
Decorate with cherries. Serves four.

Mince Pie with Apricots

Ingredients
6 oz self-raising flour
3 rounded tablespoons powdered skimmed milk

1½ rounded tablespoons caster sugar
pinch of salt
½ jar mincemeat (p. 48)
11 oz tin apricots

Method
Sieve all the dry ingredients together, adding enough water
to form a dough. Roll out on a floured board and line an
8-inch pie plate. Spread the mincemeat over the pastry and
cover with drained and chopped apricots together with 2
tablespoons apricot juice. Cover with remaining pastry,
brush with liquid skimmed milk and sprinkle with sugar.
Bake in a preheated oven (375°F (190°C) or Gas Mark 5) for
25 minutes. Serves four to six.

Potato and Apple Tart

Ingredients
3 rounded tablespoons cold mashed potato
1 medium eating apple, peeled and cored
4 tablespoons caster sugar
4 tablespoons self-raising flour
3 tablespoons powdered skimmed milk

Method
Put the mashed potato into a bowl and add 2 tablespoons
sugar and beat with a fork until a fine creamy mixture is
formed. Add the powdered skimmed milk and gradually
stir in the flour, 1 tablespoon at a time, until the mixture
resembles a fine dough. Divide into 2 pieces. Roll out 1
piece on a generously floured surface and form a circle to fit

a non-stick sponge tin. Grate the apple over the potato mixture and sprinkle with 1 tablespoon sugar. Roll the remaining dough to the same size and cover the apple. Sprinkle with remaining sugar. Bake in a preheated oven 375°F (190°C) or Gas Mark 5) for 25 to 30 minutes. Allow to cool slightly but cover with a clean cloth to steam. Serve warm. Serves four to six.

Raspberry Medley

Ingredients
3 large egg whites
4 oz caster sugar
2 oz ground rice
½ teaspoon vanilla essence
½ lb raspberries sweetened to taste, or
   7¾ oz tin raspberries

Mock cream
3 teaspoons cornflour
¼ pint liquid skimmed milk
1 dessertspoon caster sugar
2 tablespoons powdered skimmed milk
½ teaspoon vanilla essence

Method
Whisk egg whites until stiff. Gradually fold in the sugar and ground rice and finally the vanilla essence. Cut 2 7-inch rounds of vegetable parchment or rice paper and place shiny side down on 2 swiss-roll trays. Divide mixture equally and spread to within ½ inch of the edge of the paper. Bake in a

preheated oven (300°F (150°C) or Gas Mark 2) for 45 minutes. Leave in an open oven to cool. Make the mock cream by blending the cornflour, sugar and powdered milk with a little liquid milk. Add vanilla essence and stir. Heat the remaining milk in a saucepan and add to the cornflour blend. Stir, and return to the pan until the mixture comes to the boil. Remove from heat, stirring frequently until the cream is cold. Beat thoroughly. Drain raspberries, if tinned. Remove paper from the meringues and spread each with cream. Sandwich with raspberries, reserving a few for decoration, and chill for 2 hours before serving. Serves four.

Rhubarb Relish

Ingredients
1 lb fresh rhubarb, or 1 large tin rhubarb
sugar to sweeten fresh fruit
2 oz semolina
2 oz sugar
1 pint liquid skimmed milk
2 standard (No. 3 size) egg whites
3 oz caster sugar

Method
If using fresh rhubarb, sweeten to taste and simmer until tender. Place fruit in the bottom of a casserole. Make a paste with the semolina and 2 oz sugar mixed together with a little milk from the pint. Bring remainder of milk to the boil and pour on to the paste, return to the pan and bring back to the boil for 3 to 4 minutes. Pour gently on to the rhubarb and leave to cool. Meanwhile, whisk the egg whites until stiff

and forming peaks, gradually folding in the caster sugar a little at a time. Place on the semolina mixture and bake in a preheated oven (350°F (180°C) or Gas Mark 4) for 10 to 15 minutes or until meringue is golden brown. Serves four.

Spicy Bread Pudding

Ingredients
¼ lb mixed dried fruit
6 slices bread
1 teaspoon mixed spice
3 oz + 1 dessertspoon Demerara sugar
1 pint liquid skimmed milk

Method
Trim crusts from bread and cut into small pieces. Place in a bowl and add 3 oz Demerara sugar, spice and fruit. Add the milk and mix thoroughly. Turn into an ovenproof dish and sprinkle with the remaining sugar. Place in a preheated oven (400°F (200°C) or Gas Mark 6) and bake for 30 minutes. Serves four.

Strawberry Crunch

Ingredients
14 oz tin strawberry pie filling, or
1 lb fresh strawberries ⎫
3 tablespoons sugar   ⎬
3 tablespoons water   ⎭

Topping
2 oz Rice Krispies
2 tablespoons powdered skimmed milk
1 tablespoon brown sugar
1 tablespoon syrup from a warmed spoon
1 tablespoon hot water to mix

Method
If using fresh fruit, gently simmer in water and sweeten to
taste and allow to cool. Place fruit or pie filling in an
ovenproof dish. Mix the ingredients of the topping
together, bind with syrup and water and spread over fruit.
Bake in a preheated oven (425°F (220°C) or Gas Mark 7) for
15 to 20 minutes. Can be served alone or with custard.
Serves four.

Sweet Mincemeat Roly Poly

Ingredients
6 oz self-raising flour
3 rounded tablespoons powdered skimmed milk
1½ rounded tablespoons caster sugar
pinch of salt
water to mix
½ jar mincemeat (see p. 48)
a few drops Grand Marnier (optional)
1 teaspoon caster sugar

Method
Sieve dry ingredients together and mix with water to form a
dough. Roll out on a floured board into an oblong shape

approximately ¼-inch thick. Spread generously with mincemeat to within 1 inch of edge of pastry and sprinkle with Grand Marnier if liked. Brush edges with milk and roll up. Sprinkle with caster sugar and bake in a preheated oven (375°F (190°C) or Gas Mark 5) for 25 minutes. Serves four.

Treacle Tart

Ingredients
PASTRY
4 rounded tablespoons self-raising flour
1 dessertspoon caster sugar
2 rounded tablespoons powdered skimmed milk
pinch of salt
water

FILLING
6 slices of bread made into crumbs
3 tablespoons syrup from a warmed spoon
1 teaspoon lemon essence or fresh lemon juice
1 dessertspoon custard powder

Method
To make pastry sieve the dry ingredients together adding enough water to form a soft dough. Line a flan dish with pastry. Place the breadcrumbs in a bowl and stir in the custard powder, syrup and lemon juice. Spread carefully over pastry and bake in a preheated oven (375°F (190°C) or Gas Mark 5) for 25 minutes. Serves four.

Sweets: Refrigerated

Blackcurrant Blancmange

Ingredients
¼ lb blackcurrants
3 tablespoons water
3 oz granulated sugar
2 rounded tablespoons cornflour
2 oz granulated sugar
1 pint liquid skimmed milk
2 standard (No. 3 size) egg whites

Method
Place the blackcurrants, water and 3 oz sugar into a saucepan and boil until tender. Sieve or liquidise and leave to cool. Meanwhile mix the cornflour, 2 oz sugar and a little liquid milk to form a paste and bring remainder of the milk to the boil. Add to the cornflour, stir and return to heat and cook gently for 2 to 3 minutes. Allow to cool. Whisk the egg whites until stiff. Stir the fruit purée into the blancmange and fold in the egg whites. Pour into desired dish and chill in the refrigerator. Serves four.

Coffee Mandarin Crunch

Ingredients
11 oz tin mandarin oranges
1 packet orange jelly
4 tablespoons powdered skimmed milk
3 oz cornflakes
4 level tablespoons golden syrup
2 teaspoons coffee powder

Method
Drain oranges and, reserving juice, place on desired dish leaving 4 segments aside for decoration. Measure juice and then make up to ½ pint with water. Put jelly into a saucepan, add juice and place on a low heat until melted. Do not boil. Cool until almost set. Place the powdered milk into a bowl with ⅓ pint water and whisk until thick and creamy, add the jelly and whisk again. Pour carefully on to the orange and leave to set. Place syrup in a saucepan, warm and add cornflakes and coffee powder. Stir until flakes are coated and pour on to a plate to cool. Arrange on top of the jelly. Decorate with remaining segments to form a flower. Will keep covered in a refrigerator for several days. Serves four to six.

Raspberry Mousse

Ingredients
7¾ oz tin raspberries
1 packet raspberry jelly or crystals
½ pint liquid skimmed milk
water

Method
Strain the fruit, increasing the juice to ½ pint with water.
Bring to the boil and pour over jelly. Stir until dissolved.
Add the raspberries and liquid milk and whisk thoroughly
before placing in a wetted mould. Cool and place in a
refrigerator until nearly set. Remove, repeat whisking and
return to the refrigerator until set. Serves three.

Strawberry Sponge

Ingredients
4 tablespoons strawberry jam
1 packet strawberry jelly
8 thin slices bread, trimmed

Method
Spread the bread generously with strawberry jam, sandwich
slices together and place in a 1-pint pudding basin in layers
until full. Make the jelly according to the instructions on the
packet and when cold, but not set, carefully spoon on to the
bread until all the jelly is absorbed. Place a cover on top of
the basin and chill in the refrigerator for 24 hours. Serve
with mock cream. Serves four.

Vanilla Ice Cream

Ingredients
½ pint liquid skimmed milk
1 rounded tablespoon icing sugar
1 rounded tablespoon custard powder
2 rounded tablespoons powdered skimmed milk
2 large (No. 1 size) egg whites
few drops vanilla essence

Method
Mix sugar, custard powder and powdered milk together
with a little liquid milk to form a paste. Bring remainder of
the milk to the boil, pour on to the custard powder mixture
and stir well. Return to the saucepan and boil for 1 minute.
Cool. Meanwhile, whisk the egg whites until stiff, add
vanilla essence and fold into the custard when cold. Pour
into a suitable dish, cover and place in the freezer for 15 to
20 minutes until mixture is starting to set round the edges.
Whisk ice cream once again to break down the ice crystals,
then freeze until hard. Remove from the freezer 10 minutes
before using. Serves three.

Substitute Whipped Cream

Ingredients
1 pint liquid powdered skimmed milk
pinch of salt
½ oz gelatine
2 rounded tablespoons powdered skimmed milk

1 rounded tablespoon custard powder
2-3 oz caster sugar, according to taste
3 drops vanilla essence

Method
Dissolve the gelatine in a little water in a bowl standing in a pan of warm water over a moderate heat. Add the powdered milk and custard powder blended with 4 tablespoons of liquid skimmed milk. Heat the remaining milk with a pinch of salt until it is boiling and stir into the mixture in the bowl. Return to pan and boil for 1 to 2 minutes. Add the sugar and essence. When mixture is cold but not set, whisk it thoroughly until the cream has risen considerably and is light. Chill before using.

Cakes

Afternoon Tea Scone

Ingredients
4 rounded tablespoons self-raising flour
2 level tablespoons powdered skimmed milk
1 level dessertspoon caster sugar
$\frac{1}{2}$ level teaspoon cream of tartar
1 tablespoon sultanas
1 egg white
little liquid skimmed milk
pinch of salt

Method
Sieve dry ingredients together. Whisk egg white and stir into the mixture with the sultanas. Add a little liquid milk to make a soft dough. Roll out to $\frac{1}{2}$-inch thickness and mark with a cross. Transfer to a non-stick baking sheet and bake in a preheated oven (450°F (230°C) or Gas Mark 8) for 10 to 15 minutes. Spread with jam and eat while warm.

Apple Cake

Ingredients
6 oz self-raising flour
3½ oz Demerara sugar
2 oz powdered skimmed milk
½ teaspoon cinnamon
2 standard (No. 3 size) egg whites
1 tablespoon honey
1 tablespoon liquid skimmed milk
3 oz sultanas
1 large apple
pinch of salt

Method
Sieve flour, milk, salt and cinnamon together and stir in the sugar. Whisk egg whites until frothy and add to dry mixture with the honey and liquid milk. Stir in the sultanas. Peel, core and shred the apple and fold into the mixture. Pour into a 1 lb non-stick loaf tin and bake in a preheated oven (375°F (190°C) or Gas Mark 5) for 30 minutes, reducing heat to moderately slow (325°F or Gas Mark 3) for a further 20 minutes.

Apricot Gateau

Ingredients
1 packet fatless plain sponge mix
2 large (No. 1 size) egg whites
1 teaspoon custard powder
3 tablespoons powdered skimmed milk
½ pint whipped cream (see p. 76)

Decoration
1 15 oz can apricot halves
2 tablespoons apricot jam
7 glacé cherries

Method
Lightly flour a non-stick swiss-roll tin. Put the sponge mix, custard powder and powdered milk into a bowl and mix well together. Whisk egg whites until frothy and add to the mixture. Stir until a smooth consistency is reached and pour into prepared tin and bake according to instructions on the sponge mix packet, (normally 400°F (200°C) or Gas Mark 6) for 10 to 15 minutes. Allow to cool before removing from tin. When sponge is cold, cut into three equal pieces. Drain apricots and mash 3 halves together with 2 tablespoons whipped cream. Spread on to 1 layer of the cake. Cover with a second layer, repeat filling, and cover with third layer. Decorate the sides of the sponge with the remaining cream. Warm the apricot jam and spread on top of the sponge and, using 10 apricot halves, form 2 rows along the centre of the gateau, placing the cherries in the centre of the apricots. Put in the refrigerator until set. This gateau can then be served. To keep for further use, cover with seal and replace in the refrigerator. Will keep for several days.

Banana Cake

Ingredients
3 ripe bananas, peeled
3 rounded tablespoons + 1 teaspoon brown sugar
pinch of salt
2 standard (No. 3 size) egg whites

6 oz self-raising flour
1 teaspoon lemon juice
4 rounded tablespoons powdered skimmed milk
½ teaspoon banana essence
½ teaspoon bicarbonate of soda

Method
Mash the bananas with salt and 3 rounded tablespoons of sugar. Add lemon juice and milk and beat well. Sieve the flour and bicarbonate of soda and add to the banana mixture a little at a time with the beaten egg whites and banana essence. Turn into an 8-inch non-stick sponge tin. Sprinkle with remaining 1 teaspoon sugar and bake in a preheated oven (350°F (180°C) or Gas Mark 4) for 40 minutes.

Boiled Cake

Ingredients
6 oz sultanas
¾ cup cold water
½ teaspoon bicarbonate of soda
1 oz mixed peel
¾ cup granulated sugar
1 dessertspoon honey
2 large (No. 1 size) egg whites
1 cup self-raising flour
3 tablespoons powdered skimmed milk

Method
Pour the water into a saucepan and add sugar, sultanas, peel, bicarbonate of soda and honey and bring gently to the boil, stirring until the sugar dissolves. Continue to boil for a

few minutes and set aside to cool. Whisk egg whites until frothy and fold into the mixture together with the flour and milk. Pour into a 1 lb non-stick loaf tin and level cake mixture with a knife. Place on the middle shelf of a preheated oven (350°F (180°C) or Gas Mark 4) for 40 to 45 minutes. Will keep for four days.

Cherry-topped Cake

Ingredients
6 oz self-raising flour
3 oz Demerara sugar
3 oz sultanas or raisins
1 oz mixed peel
pinch of salt
3 tablespoons skimmed milk
2 large (No. 1 size) egg whites
1 dessertspoon honey
1 teaspoon almond essence
2–3 tablespoons liquid skimmed milk
9 cherries, halved

Method
Sieve flour, salt and powdered milk and stir in sugar, peel and dried fruit. Whisk egg whites until frothy and add to the mixture together with the honey, liquid milk and almond essence. Turn into a 1 lb non-stick loaf tin. Cut the cherries in halves and place in rows on top of the cake. Bake in a preheated oven (325°F (160°C) or Gas Mark 3) for 30 to 40 minutes.

Date and Apple Cake

Ingredients
¼ lb cooking apples, peeled and sliced
2 tablespoons water
1 tablespoon caster sugar
6 oz self-raising flour
3 oz Demerara sugar
pinch of salt
3 tablespoons powdered skimmed milk
3 oz chopped dates
1 dessertspoon honey
2 tablespoons liquid skimmed milk

Method
Cook the apples with the water and caster sugar until soft, and set aside to cool. Sieve flour, salt and powdered milk together. Add the Demerara sugar and dates and mix well. Beat in the honey, apple and liquid milk. Pour into a 7-inch non-stick sponge tin and bake in a preheated oven (375°F (190°C) Gas Mark 5) for 30 minutes. Will keep for four days.

Date and Ginger Cake

Ingredients
4½ oz self-raising flour
2 tablespoons powdered skimmed milk
2 oz + 1 teaspoon Demerara sugar
1 level tablespoon golden syrup from a warmed spoon
½ level teaspoon ground ginger

4 oz stoned dates, chopped
1 oz mixed peel
1 large (No. 1 size) egg white
3 tablespoons liquid skimmed milk
pinch of salt

Method
Sieve together flour, powdered milk, salt and ground ginger
and add 2 oz sugar and the warmed syrup. Whisk egg white
until frothy and add to the mixture together with the fruit
and liquid milk and mix thoroughly. Pour into a 7-inch
non-stick sandwich tin, sprinkle the 1 teaspoon sugar on
top and bake in a preheated oven (350°F (180°C) or Gas
Mark 4) for 45 to 50 minutes.

Date and Orange Cake

Ingredients
$\frac{1}{2}$ 11oz tin mandarin oranges
$\frac{1}{4}$ lb stoned dates, chopped
1 tablespoon honey from a warmed spoon
6 oz self-raising flour
3 oz caster sugar
3 tablespoons powdered skimmed milk
1 teaspoon ground ginger
2 standard (No. 3 size) egg whites
1 tablespoon liquid skimmed milk
pinch of salt

Method
Sieve flour, salt, sugar, powdered milk and ginger together.
Drain oranges and cut into small pieces and add together
with the dates to the dried mixture. Whisk egg whites until
frothy and add with the liquid milk to the mixture and stir
thoroughly. Place in a 1 lb non-stick loaf tin and bake in a
preheated oven (375°F (190°C) or Gas Mark 5) for 40 to 45
minutes.

Family Fruit Cake

Ingredients
8 oz self-raising flour
pinch of salt
$\frac{1}{4}$ teaspoon nutmeg
$\frac{1}{4}$ teaspoon cinnamon
$\frac{1}{2}$ level teaspoon mixed spice
4 tablespoons powdered skimmed milk
3 oz brown sugar
3 oz currants
3 oz sultanas
2 oz stoned dates, chopped
1 oz glacé cherries, chopped
1 teaspoon lemon essence
$\frac{1}{4}$ pint (approx) liquid skimmed milk

Method
Sieve dry ingredients together and stir in sugar and various
fruits and mix well together. Make a hollow in the centre of
the mixture and add the lemon essence and half the liquid

milk. Gradually add the remaining milk until the mixture forms a soft consistency. Transfer to a 1 lb non-stick loaf tin and bake in a preheated oven (375°F (190°C) or Gas Mark 5) for 30 minutes, reducing heat (325°F (160°C) or Gas Mark 3) for a further 30 minutes. This cake improves with keeping.

Ginger Fruit Cake

Ingredients
6 oz self-raising flour
1 level teaspoon ground ginger
pinch of salt
$\frac{1}{4}$ teaspoon cinnamon
4 level tablespoons powdered skimmed milk
2 oz dark brown sugar
1 cup mixed fruit
2 large (No. 1 size) egg whites
5 tablespoons liquid skimmed milk
1 heaped tablespoon black treacle from a warmed spoon

Method
Sieve all dry ingredients together with the exception of the sugar. Stir in the fruit and sugar. Whisk egg whites and add to the mixture with the liquid milk and warmed treacle. Place in an 8-inch non-stick sandwich tin and cook in a preheated oven (375°F (190°C) or Gas Mark 5) for 20 to 25 minutes. This cake improves with keeping.

Ginger Triangles

Ingredients
5 oz self-raising flour
3 tablespoons powdered skimmed milk
¼ teaspoon bicarbonate of soda
1 rounded teaspoon ground ginger
pinch of salt
2 oz + 2 oz Demerara sugar
2 large (No. 1 size) egg whites
1 tablespoon black treacle from a warmed spoon
2 tablespoons liquid skimmed milk

Method
Sieve flour, milk, bicarbonate of soda, ginger and salt together and stir in 2 oz sugar. Beat the egg whites until frothy and add to the mixture together with the treacle and liquid skimmed milk. Turn into a 7-inch non-stick sponge tin and sprinkle with remaining sugar. Bake in a preheated oven (375°F (190°C) or Gas Mark 5) for 15 to 20 minutes. Cut into triangles when cold. Will keep for three days.

Nutty Cake

Ingredients
2 crushed Weetabix
1 tablespoon brown sugar
2 oz self-raising flour
2 tablespoons powdered skimmed milk
1 tablespoon syrup from a warmed spoon
4 tablespoons liquid skimmed milk

Method

Crush the Weetabix until forming fine crumbs and add the remaining dry ingredients. Stir in the warmed syrup and liquid milk and pour into a 7-inch non-stick sandwich tin. Bake in a preheated oven (375°F (190°C) or Gas Mark 5) for 25 minutes.

Oat, Sultana and Cherry Triangles

Ingredients

8 oz quick cooking oats
2 oz brown sugar
4 tablespoons powdered skimmed milk
pinch of salt
2 tablespoons syrup from a warmed spoon
4 oz sultanas
2 oz glacé cherries, chopped
1 tablespoon lemon juice
2–4 tablespoons liquid skimmed milk

Method

Place all dry ingredients into a basin and mix well. Stir in the sultanas, cherries, syrup and lemon juice and enough milk for the mixture to be a dropping consistency. Place in a 7-inch non-stick sponge tin and bake in a preheated oven (400°F (200°C) or Gas Mark 6) for 25 minutes. Cut into triangles when cold.

Orange Refrigerator Sponge

Ingredients
1 packet fatless plain sponge mix
1 dessertspoon honey
2 large (No. 1 size) egg whites, beaten
grated rind of 1 orange
3 tablespoons powdered skimmed milk
1 teaspoon custard powder
pinch of salt
2 tablespoons liquid skimmed milk
2 tablespoons orange marmalade
¼ pint whipped cream (see p. 76)

Method
Empty the sponge mix into a bowl with salt, custard powder and powdered milk, and mix together. Add honey, grated orange rind and beaten egg whites and stir in liquid milk. Mix well and divide equally between 2 non-stick sponge tins. Bake in a preheated oven (400°F (200°C) or Gas Mark 6) for 10 to 15 minutes. Remove to a cooling tray and when cold spread the marmalade and whipped cream over the sponges and sandwich together. Dredge with icing sugar if liked. This sponge should be eaten within four days. In the meantime this sponge should be kept in the refrigerator, covered with stretch-and-seal paper.

Peppermint Cake

Ingredients
3 oz cornflakes, crushed
2 oz self-raising flour
1 oz brown sugar
2 oz stoned dates, chopped
2–3 drops peppermint essence
2 large (No. 1 size) egg whites
1 level tablespoon honey from a warmed spoon
liquid skimmed milk to bind

ICING
4 tablespoons icing sugar, sifted
2 drops peppermint essence
1 dessertspoon warm water

Method
Whisk egg whites with 2 drops of peppermint essence until stiff. Crush cornflakes and add all other dry ingredients and fold in peppermint and egg whites. Add the warmed honey and a little milk to make a soft consistency. Place in a 7-inch non-stick sandwich tin and bake in a preheated oven (375°F (190°C) or Gas Mark 5) for 15 to 20 minutes. Mix together icing sugar, peppermint essence and warm water and spread on cake when it is cold. Will keep for two or three days.

Raisin, Date and Ginger Cake

Ingredients
2 oz Rice Krispies
2 oz stoned dates, chopped
2 oz raisins
1 level teaspoon ground ginger
2 oz self-raising flour
1 oz brown sugar
3 tablespoons powdered skimmed milk
1 tablespoon honey from a warmed spoon
5 tablespoons liquid skimmed milk

Method
Mix all dry ingredients together and thoroughly stir in the liquid milk and warmed honey. Spread into a 7-inch non-stick sandwich tin and bake in a preheated oven (375°F (190°C) or Gas Mark 5) for 25 to 30 minutes.

Rock Buns

Ingredients
8 oz self-raising flour
4 tablespoons powdered skimmed milk
3 oz + 1 teaspoon caster sugar
½ teaspoon mixed spice
pinch of salt
1 large (No. 1 size) egg white
5 tablespoons liquid skimmed milk
3 oz mixed cake fruit

Method

Sieve dry ingredients together and add 3 oz sugar with the fruit and mix well. Beat the egg white with the milk and add to the mixture, stirring thoroughly. Spoon into small heaps on a non-stick baking tray. Sprinkle with remaining sugar and bake in a preheated oven (425°F (220°C) or Gas Mark 7) for 10 to 15 minutes.

Simnel Cake

Ingredients
8 oz mixed fruit
1 oz glacé cherries, chopped
1 oz mixed peel
1 level teaspoon mixed spice
3 oz soft brown sugar
3 tablespoons powdered skimmed milk
1 tablespoon marmalade
5 oz self-raising flour
1 tablespoon sherry
2 large (No. 1 size) egg whites
1 dessertspoon black treacle from a warmed spoon
liquid skimmed milk

MOCK MARZIPAN
4 oz semolina
4 oz icing sugar, sifted
1 dessertspoon custard powder
1 standard (No. 3 size) egg white, beaten
2 teaspoons almond essence

Method
Sieve dry ingredients together. Stir in fruit and sugar and add marmalade, sherry and warmed treacle. Whisk the egg whites until frothy and gradually beat into the mixture with a little liquid milk. Place half the mixture into an 8-inch non-stick cake tin and spread evenly. Meanwhile, mix the semolina, icing sugar and custard powder and add the beaten egg white and essence. Blend together to form a firm paste. Roll out and cut to the size of the tin and place on top of the cake mixture. Place the remaining mixture on top of the mock marzipan, hollow out the centre and bake in a preheated oven (325°F (160°C) or Gas Mark 3) for 2 hours. Will keep for two weeks.

Spicy Apple Cake

Ingredients
1 large cooking apple
8 oz self-raising flour
3 tablespoons powdered skimmed milk
1 level teaspoon ground ginger
1 level teaspoon cinnamon
1 level teaspoon mixed spice
3 oz + 2 teaspoons caster sugar
4 oz sultanas or raisins
liquid skimmed milk to mix

ICING
2 tablespoons icing sugar, sifted
water to mix

Method

Peel, core and slice apple and add 2 teaspoons sugar and a little water and simmer gently until soft. Set aside to cool. Sieve all dry ingredients together and stir in 3 oz sugar, fruit, cooked apple and a little liquid milk to make a soft consistency. Place into a 1 lb non-stick loaf tin and bake in a preheated oven (400°F (200°C) or Gas Mark 6) for 20 minutes, reducing temperature (325°F (160°C) or Gas Mark 3) for a further 20 minutes. Leave to cool in the tin for 30 minutes, turn out on to a cooling tray and, when cold, mix the icing sugar with a little cold water and spread over the top of the cake. Will keep fresh for a week.

Glossary of English Terms with some American Equivalents

The following equivalents and explanations may be useful to anyone not familiar with English usage. The list of Dos and Don'ts on page 11 must be strictly observed. All packets must be looked at carefully to ensure that the contents listed do not include any of the forbidden items. This is particularly important for cake mixes and gravy and bouillon cubes.

Angelica	The candied stem and root of an aromatic plant used for decorating cakes, puddings, etc.
Baking powder	American baking powder may be stronger than the British variety and less will be needed—possibly only half the amount specified
Basin	In these recipes, a pudding bowl in which the pudding can be boiled or steamed
Beef	'Skirt' or 'chuck' of beef signifies stewing steak; 'topside' is akin to rump roast
Bicarbonate of soda	Baking soda
Black treacle	Molasses may be substituted

Butter beans	Large, dried white-seeded beans similar to Lima beans
Caster sugar	Fine granular, white sugar suitable for use in a sugar caster or sifter—used because it blends and dissolves more readily than coarser sugars
Channel Island milk	Milk from the Jersey and Guernsey breeds of cattle which is especially rich in milk fat
Chicken joint	A complete limb of a chicken—a chicken piece
Cornflour	Cornstarch
Custard powder	Proprietary item based on cornstarch and containing no eggs or milk fat
Demerara sugar	A golden-coloured crystalline form of sugar
Dried herbs	A mixture of dried, savoury herbs—a typical example might contain sage, thyme, marjoram and pennyroyal
Flour	Where plain flour is specified all purpose flour should be used. In Britain, self-raising flour contains added baking powder. 'Saffron flour' is a proprietary item coloured and flavoured with saffron. 'Seasoned flour' in these recipes means flour to which salt and pepper have been added before using it
Frying pan	Skillet
Glacé cherries	Candied, whole, stoned cherries
Golden Raising Powder	A proprietary brand of coloured baking powder

Golden syrup	A sugar syrup more highly refined than black treacle
Gravy browning/powder	A proprietary item for thickening and colouring gravy
Ground rice	A granular form of rice flour
Icing sugar	Confectioners' sugar
Loaf tin	Bread baking tin
Minced meat	Ground meat (not to be confused, of course, with mincemeat described on p. 48)
Mixed fruit	Dried raisins, currants and sultanas, bought ready mixed
Mixed peel	Candied orange and lemon peel bought mixed and chopped ready for use
Mixed spice	The common spices bought ready ground and mixed. A typical example might contain cinnamon, coriander, dill, fennel, nutmeg, ginger, clove, turmeric
Orange squash	Orange juice
Packet of jelly	Fruit-flavoured gelatine in crystalline or cake form which only needs to be dissolved in boiling water
Patty tin	A tin for baking a batch of small pies or cakes each in its own mould—a cupcake tin
Sandwich tin	A 'layer cake pan' either round or oblong
Sultana	A dried, seedless raisin, originally from Smyrna, usually lighter in colour than ordinary dried raisins

Tart	Usually, an open fruit pie
Tomato purée	Tomato paste
Worcestershire sauce	A proprietary bottled sauce used for flavouring stews, etc.
Whiting	A small, white-fleshed sea fish

Index